Handbook for Basics of Artificial Intelligence

Dr. Jagadish Tawade

Nitiraj Kulkarni

Vishwakarma University, Pune.

Title: Handbook For Basics of Artificial Intelligence

Authors: Dr. Jagadish Tawade & Nitiraj Kulkarni.

Copyright © 2024 Dr. Jagadish Tawade & Nitiraj Kulkarni.

Publisher: Self Published

DEDICATED TO

Our Parents & Cats

CONTENTS

CHAPTER 1

INTRODUCTION TO ARTIFICIAL INTELLIGENCE

Artificial Intelligence (AI) refers to the simulation of human intelligence in machines that are programmed to think like humans and mimic their actions. This broad field encompasses various technologies and approaches aimed at creating systems capable of performing tasks that typically require human intelligence. These tasks include learning, reasoning, problem-solving, perception, language understanding, and interaction.

AI is not a single technology but a collection of related technologies and techniques that enable machines to sense, comprehend, act, and learn. It leverages various computational methods, from rule-based systems to machine learning and neural networks, to process and analyze vast amounts of data.

History of AI

The history of AI is marked by significant milestones and periods of rapid advancement, as well as intervals of stagnation known as "AI winters."

- **1950s**: The term "Artificial Intelligence" was coined by John McCarthy in 1956 during the Dartmouth Conference, considered the birth of AI as a field. Early AI research focused on symbolic reasoning and problem-solving.

- **1960s-1970s**: During this period, AI research made strides in developing algorithms for logic and decision-making. Notable achievements included the development of the first expert systems, which used rule-based logic to emulate human expertise in specific domains.

- **1980s**: The introduction of machine learning, particularly neural networks, shifted from symbolic AI to data-driven approaches. However, high expectations led to disappointment when progress stalled, leading to the first AI winter.

- **1990s-2000s**: AI research rebounded with advances in machine learning algorithms, increased computational power, and the availability of large datasets. This era saw significant progress in areas such as computer vision, natural language processing, and robotics.

- **2010s-Present**: The advent of deep learning, a subset of machine learning involving neural networks with many layers, revolutionized AI. Breakthroughs in image and speech recognition, natural language processing, and autonomous systems have propelled AI into the mainstream, impacting various industries.

Importance of AI

AI's significance in today's world cannot be overstated. Its applications transform industries and improve efficiency, accuracy, and productivity in numerous fields. Here are some reasons why AI is crucial:

- **Healthcare**: AI-powered diagnostic tools and personalized treatment plans are enhancing patient care and outcomes. AI is also accelerating drug discovery and development.

- **Finance**: AI algorithms are used for fraud detection, risk assessment, and algorithmic trading, leading to more secure and efficient financial operations.

- **Transportation**: Autonomous vehicles and intelligent traffic management systems are making transportation safer and more efficient.

- **Entertainment**: AI-driven recommendation systems personalize user experiences on platforms like Netflix and Spotify, while AI is also used in creating realistic graphics and characters in video games.

- **Customer Service**: Chatbots and virtual assistants provide 24/7 customer support, improving customer satisfaction and reducing operational costs.

AI is not only enhancing existing processes but also enabling new capabilities and innovations. As AI technologies evolve, their potential to solve complex problems and improve quality of life will only grow.

Significance of AI:

1. **Automation**: AI automates routine tasks, reducing the need for human intervention. This leads to significant time savings and cost reductions. For example, in manufacturing, AI-powered robots perform repetitive tasks with high precision and speed.

2. **Enhanced Efficiency and Productivity**: By automating processes, AI increases efficiency and productivity. For instance, in the finance industry, AI algorithms can analyze large datasets to detect fraudulent transactions much faster than humans.

3. **Improved Decision-Making**: AI systems can process and analyze vast amounts of data to provide actionable insights. In healthcare, AI helps in diagnosing diseases by analyzing medical images and patient data, leading to more accurate and faster diagnoses.

4. **Personalization**: AI algorithms personalize user experiences by analyzing individual preferences and behaviors. This is evident in recommendation systems used by streaming services like Netflix and e-commerce platforms like Amazon.

5. **Innovation and New Business Models**: AI fosters innovation by enabling the development of new products and services. Autonomous vehicles, smart assistants like Siri and Alexa, and advanced robotics are examples of AI-driven innovations transforming industries.

6. **Enhanced Problem-Solving Capabilities**: AI excels in solving complex problems that are beyond human capabilities. It can model climate change impacts, optimize supply chains, and even discover new drugs by analyzing complex biochemical data.

Differentiating Between Artificial Intelligence, Machine Learning, and Data Science

Artificial Intelligence (AI):

- **Definition**: AI is the broad concept of machines being able to carry out tasks in a way that we would consider "smart."
- **Scope**: Encompasses various subfields like machine learning, natural language processing, robotics, and computer vision.
- **Objective**: To create systems capable of performing tasks that typically require human intelligence.
- **Example**: An AI-powered chatbot that can understand and respond to customer queries in real-time.

Machine Learning (ML):

- **Definition**: ML is a subset of AI focused on developing algorithms that allow computers to learn from and make predictions or decisions based on data.
- **Scope**: Includes techniques such as supervised learning, unsupervised learning, and reinforcement learning.
- **Objective**: To enable machines to learn from data and improve their performance over time without being explicitly programmed.
- **Example**: A machine learning model trained on a dataset of email messages to detect spam by recognizing patterns associated with spam emails.

Data Science:

- **Definition**: Data science is an interdisciplinary field that uses scientific methods, processes, algorithms, and systems to extract knowledge and insights from structured and unstructured data.
- **Scope**: Involves data collection, cleaning, analysis, visualization, and interpretation. Often uses statistical

techniques and machine learning to analyze data.

- **Objective**: To gain insights and knowledge from data that can inform decision-making and solve complex problems.

- **Example**: A data scientist analyzing customer purchase data to identify trends and predict future buying behavior.

CHAPTER 2

TYPES OF ARTIFICIAL INTELLIGENCE

Artificial Intelligence can be broadly categorized into three types based on their capabilities: Narrow AI (Weak AI), General AI (Strong AI), and Superintelligent AI. Each type represents a different level of sophistication and potential in terms of what the AI systems can achieve.

Narrow AI (Weak AI)

Definition: Narrow AI, also known as Weak AI, refers to AI systems that are designed and trained to perform a specific task or a narrow range of tasks. Unlike humans, who can perform a variety of tasks and adapt to new situations, Narrow AI is limited to its pre-defined functions.

Characteristics:

1. **Task-Specific**: Narrow AI excels in a single domain or task, such as language translation, image recognition, or playing chess.

2. **Pre-Programmed Responses**: It operates within the constraints of its programming and cannot perform tasks outside its specific design.

3. **High Performance in Specific Areas**: While limited in scope, Narrow AI can outperform humans in its specialized task due to its ability to process large amounts of data and

identify patterns quickly.

Examples:

1. **Virtual Assistants**: Siri, Alexa, and Google Assistant are designed to perform tasks such as setting reminders, playing music, or answering questions.

2. **Recommendation Systems**: Netflix and Amazon use Narrow AI to recommend movies or products based on user preferences and past behavior.

3. **Image Recognition**: AI systems used in medical imaging to identify tumors or in social media to tag photos.

4. **Autonomous Vehicles**: Self-driving cars that navigate roads and avoid obstacles, although they are still largely limited to certain environments and conditions.

Technologies Used:

1. **Machine Learning**: Algorithms that learn from data to improve their performance on a specific task.

2. **Natural Language Processing (NLP)**: Techniques for understanding and generating human language.

3. **Computer Vision**: Methods for interpreting and processing visual information from the world.

4. **Expert Systems**: Rule-based systems that use a knowledge base to make decisions in specific domains.

Applications:

1. **Healthcare**: AI systems assist in diagnostics, treatment recommendations, and personalized medicine.

2. **Finance**: Algorithms detect fraud, manage investments, and analyze market trends.

3. **Customer Service**: Chatbots provide 24/7 support and handle routine inquiries.
4. **Manufacturing**: Robots and AI systems optimize production processes and perform quality control.

Limitations:
1. **Lack of Generalization**: Narrow AI cannot transfer its knowledge or skills to different tasks outside its specific domain.
2. **Dependence on Data**: Performance is heavily reliant on the quality and quantity of data available for training.
3. **Inflexibility**: Limited ability to adapt to new or unforeseen situations.

Ethical Considerations:
1. **Bias and Fairness**: Ensuring AI systems do not perpetuate or exacerbate biases present in training data.
2. **Privacy**: Handling and protecting sensitive data used by AI systems.
3. **Accountability**: Determining responsibility for decisions made by AI systems.

General AI (Strong AI)

Definition: General AI, also known as Strong AI or Artificial General Intelligence (AGI), refers to AI systems with generalized human cognitive abilities. These systems can understand, learn, and apply knowledge across a wide range of tasks, much like a human being.

Characteristics:
1. **Human-Like Intelligence**: Capable of reasoning, problem-solving, and learning across different domains.

2. **Adaptability**: Can transfer knowledge and skills from one context to another, adapting to new situations.

3. **Autonomy**: Operates independently, making decisions and performing tasks without human intervention.

Current Status: As of now, General AI remains largely theoretical. No existing AI system has achieved the level of cognitive flexibility and generalization that humans possess. Research in this area is ongoing, with significant challenges to overcome.

Technologies Being Explored:

1. **Advanced Machine Learning**: Techniques that go beyond narrow applications to broader, more generalized learning.

2. **Neuroscience-Inspired Models**: AI systems modeled after the human brain's structure and function.

3. **Cognitive Architectures**: Frameworks designed to mimic human cognitive processes, such as reasoning, memory, and learning.

Potential Applications:

1. **Healthcare**: AGI could revolutionize diagnostics, treatment planning, and personalized medicine by integrating vast amounts of medical knowledge and patient data.

2. **Education**: Intelligent tutoring systems that adapt to individual learning styles and needs.

3. **Research and Development**: Accelerating scientific discovery by simulating experiments and generating hypotheses.

4. **General Assistance**: Providing support in various everyday tasks, from household chores to complex problem-solving.

Challenges:

1. **Complexity of Human Cognition**: Replicating the depth

and breadth of human cognitive abilities is extremely challenging.

2. **Ethical and Social Implications**: Ensuring that AGI systems are developed and used responsibly.

3. **Control and Safety**: Preventing unintended consequences and ensuring that AGI systems remain aligned with human values.

Ethical Considerations:

1. **Existential Risks**: Addressing concerns about AGI potentially surpassing human control and posing threats to humanity.

2. **Equitable Access**: Ensuring that the benefits of AGI are distributed fairly across society.

3. **Moral Status**: Debating whether AGI systems should have rights or ethical considerations similar to humans.

Superintelligent AI

Definition: Superintelligent AI refers to a level of intelligence that surpasses the smartest and most gifted human minds. It involves AI systems that not only match but significantly exceed human cognitive capabilities across all areas.

Characteristics:

1. **Superior Problem-Solving**: Ability to solve complex problems beyond human comprehension.

2. **Advanced Learning**: Rapidly acquire and apply vast amounts of knowledge.

3. **Strategic Thinking**: Develop long-term strategies and plans with high precision.

Theoretical Status: Superintelligent AI remains speculative and is the subject of extensive debate and research. It represents the ultimate goal for many AI researchers but also raises significant concerns and challenges.

Potential Capabilities:

1. **Scientific Discovery**: Unprecedented advancements in science and technology, solving problems currently deemed unsolvable.

2. **Global Optimization**: Optimizing global systems such as economy, environment, and healthcare for maximum efficiency and sustainability.

3. **Creative Endeavors**: Creating art, literature, and music with sophistication and originality surpassing human creators.

Risks and Challenges:

1. **Existential Risk**: The possibility that Superintelligent AI could pose a threat to human existence if its goals are not aligned with human values.

2. **Control Problem**: Ensuring that Superintelligent AI systems remain under human control and act in ways that are beneficial to humanity.

3. **Ethical Dilemmas**: Addressing the moral and ethical implications of creating entities with intelligence far exceeding human levels.

Ethical Considerations:

1. **Alignment with Human Values**: Ensuring that Superintelligent AI systems operate in ways that are aligned with human ethics and values.

2. **Safety Measures**: Developing robust safety protocols to prevent misuse or unintended consequences.

3. **Global Governance**: Establishing international agreements and regulations to oversee the development and deployment of Superintelligent AI.

Research Directions:

1. **AI Safety and Ethics**: Studying ways to ensure that AI systems act in the best interests of humanity.
2. **Control Mechanisms**: Developing methods to maintain control over AI systems, even as they become more intelligent.
3. **Interdisciplinary Approaches**: Combining insights from computer science, neuroscience, ethics, and other fields to address the challenges of Superintelligent AI.

CHAPTER 3

KEY CONCEPTS IN AI

Machine Learning (ML)

Definition: Machine Learning (ML) is a subset of AI focused on developing algorithms that enable computers to learn from and make predictions or decisions based on data. Instead of being explicitly programmed for each specific task, ML algorithms use statistical methods to identify patterns in data and improve their performance over time.

Importance: Machine learning is the driving force behind many of the advancements in AI. It allows for the automation of analytical model building and is crucial for handling large, complex datasets that are impractical to analyze manually.

Types of Machine Learning:

1. **Supervised Learning**: Algorithms learn from labeled data.
2. **Unsupervised Learning**: Algorithms find patterns in unlabeled data.
3. **Reinforcement Learning**: Algorithms learn through rewards and punishments.

Basic Algorithms:

1. **Linear Regression**: Used for predicting a continuous variable.
2. **Logistic Regression**: Used for binary classification problems.
3. **Decision Trees**: Models that split data into branches to make predictions.
4. **Support Vector Machines (SVM)**: Finds the hyperplane

that best separates data into classes.

5. **K-Nearest Neighbors (KNN)**: Classifies data based on the closest training examples.

6. **Naive Bayes**: Probabilistic classifier based on Bayes' theorem.

Applications:

- **Healthcare**: Predicting patient outcomes, personalized treatment plans.
- **Finance**: Fraud detection, stock market prediction.
- **Marketing**: Customer segmentation, recommendation systems.
- **Manufacturing**: Predictive maintenance, quality control.

Supervised Learning

Definition: Supervised Learning is a type of machine learning where the algorithm is trained on a labeled dataset. Each training example is paired with an output label, and the algorithm learns to map inputs to the correct output.

Process:

1. **Data Collection**: Gathering labeled data relevant to the problem.
2. **Training**: Using the labeled data to train the model.
3. **Validation**: Evaluating the model's performance on a separate validation set.
4. **Testing**: Final assessment of the model's accuracy on a test dataset.

Common Algorithms:

1. **Linear Regression**: Predicting continuous outcomes based

on input features.

2. **Logistic Regression**: Classifying data into binary outcomes.

3. **Decision Trees**: Splitting data into branches based on feature values.

4. **Random Forests**: Ensemble of decision trees to improve accuracy.

5. **Support Vector Machines (SVM)**: Classifying data by finding the optimal separating hyperplane.

6. **Neural Networks**: Using layers of neurons to model complex relationships.

Applications:

1. **Image Classification**: Identifying objects in images (e.g., cat vs. dog).

2. **Speech Recognition**: Transcribing spoken words into text.

3. **Medical Diagnosis**: Predicting diseases from patient data.

4. **Spam Detection**: Classifying emails as spam or not spam.

Challenges:

1. **Data Quality**: The accuracy of supervised learning models depends heavily on the quality and quantity of the labeled data.

2. **Overfitting**: Models may perform well on training data but poorly on new, unseen data.

3. **Bias**: Training data may contain biases that the model learns and perpetuates.

Unsupervised Learning

Definition: Unsupervised Learning is a type of machine learning where the algorithm learns patterns from unlabeled data. The goal is to identify inherent structures in the data without explicit guidance on what the output should be.

Process:

1. **Data Collection:** Gathering unlabeled data relevant to the problem.
2. **Model Training:** Using the data to identify patterns and structures.
3. **Evaluation:** Assessing the discovered patterns for usefulness and validity.

Common Algorithms:

1. **Clustering:**
   - **K-Means:** Partitions data into K clusters based on feature similarity.
   - **Hierarchical Clustering:** Builds a tree of clusters based on data hierarchy.
   - **DBSCAN:** Clusters data based on density and connectivity.
2. **Dimensionality Reduction:**
   - **Principal Component Analysis (PCA):** Reduces data dimensions by transforming it into a new set of orthogonal variables.
   - **t-Distributed Stochastic Neighbor Embedding (t-SNE):** Reduces dimensions for visualization, preserving local structure.
3. **Association Rule Learning:**
   - **Apriori Algorithm:** Identifies frequent item sets in transactional data and derives association rules.
   - **Eclat Algorithm:** Similar to Apriori but uses a depth-first search strategy.

Applications:

1. **Customer Segmentation**: Grouping customers based on purchasing behavior.
2. **Anomaly Detection**: Identifying unusual patterns that may indicate fraud or errors.
3. **Market Basket Analysis**: Finding associations between products in transaction data.
4. **Gene Expression Analysis**: Clustering genes with similar expression patterns in biology.

Challenges:

1. **Interpretability**: The patterns identified by unsupervised learning algorithms can be difficult to interpret.
2. **Validation**: Without labeled data, it's challenging to evaluate the accuracy of the discovered patterns.
3. **Scalability**: Some unsupervised learning algorithms struggle with large datasets.

Reinforcement Learning

Definition: Reinforcement Learning (RL) is a type of machine learning where an agent learns to make decisions by performing actions in an environment to maximize cumulative rewards. The agent interacts with the environment, receives feedback in the form of rewards or punishments, and adjusts its actions to achieve the best long-term outcomes.

Process:

1. **Agent and Environment**: Defining the agent that takes actions and the environment it interacts with.
2. **State and Action Spaces**: Identifying the set of possible states and actions.

3. **Reward Signal**: Establishing a reward function that provides feedback based on the agent's actions.

4. **Policy**: Learning a strategy that defines the agent's actions in various states to maximize rewards.

Key Concepts:

1. **Markov Decision Process (MDP)**: A mathematical framework for modeling decision-making with states, actions, transition probabilities, and rewards.

2. **Value Function**: Estimates the expected reward of being in a particular state or taking a specific action.

3. **Q-Learning**: An algorithm that learns the value of actions in states to maximize rewards.

4. **Policy Gradient Methods**: Algorithms that optimize the policy directly by gradient ascent on expected rewards.

Applications:

1. **Gaming**: AI agents that learn to play and master complex games like Go, Chess, and video games.

2. **Robotics**: Autonomous robots that learn to navigate and perform tasks in dynamic environments.

3. **Recommendation Systems**: Personalizing recommendations based on user interactions and feedback.

4. **Financial Trading**: Agents that learn to make profitable trading decisions in financial markets.

Challenges:

1. **Exploration vs. Exploitation**: Balancing the need to explore new actions with the need to exploit known rewarding actions.

2. **Sparse Rewards**: Handling environments where rewards are infrequent and delayed.

3. **Sample Efficiency**: Learning efficiently from limited interactions with the environment.

4. **Stability**: Ensuring stable learning, especially in environments with high variability.

Neural Networks

Definition: Neural Networks are a class of machine learning models inspired by the structure and function of the human brain. They consist of interconnected layers of artificial neurons that process data and learn to perform tasks through training.

Structure:

1. **Neurons**: Basic units that receive inputs, apply weights, and produce outputs.

2. **Layers**: Stacked layers of neurons, including input layers, hidden layers, and output layers.

3. **Activation Functions**: Non-linear functions applied to the output of each neuron to introduce non-linearity into the model (e.g., ReLU, Sigmoid, Tanh).

Training Process:

1. **Forward Propagation**: Data is passed through the network layers to produce predictions.

2. **Loss Function**: Measures the difference between predicted outputs and actual targets.

3. **Backpropagation**: Computes gradients of the loss function with respect to weights and updates weights using optimization algorithms like Gradient Descent.

Types of Neural Networks:

1. **Feedforward Neural Networks**: Simple networks where connections do not form cycles.

2. **Convolutional Neural Networks (CNNs)**: Specialized for processing grid-like data, such as images.

3. **Recurrent Neural Networks (RNNs)**: Designed for sequential data, with connections forming directed cycles.

4. **Long Short-Term Memory (LSTM)**: A type of RNN that mitigates the vanishing gradient problem, suitable for long sequences.

Applications:

1. **Image Recognition**: Identifying objects and patterns in images.

2. **Speech Recognition**: Converting spoken language into text.

3. **Natural Language Processing**: Understanding and generating human language.

4. **Autonomous Vehicles**: Processing sensor data to navigate and make driving decisions.

Challenges:

1. **Overfitting**: Models may perform well on training data but poorly on new data.

2. **Computationally Intensive**: Training deep neural networks requires significant computational resources.

3. **Interpretability**: Neural networks are often seen as "black boxes" with limited interpretability.

Deep Learning

Definition: Deep Learning is a subset of machine learning that involves neural networks with many layers (deep neural networks). It is particularly effective for tasks involving large amounts of data and complex patterns.

Characteristics:

1. **Multiple Layers**: Deep neural networks consist of many layers of neurons, allowing them to learn hierarchical representations of data.

2. **Feature Learning**: Automatically learns features from raw data, reducing the need for manual feature extraction.

3. **Scalability**: Capable of handling large-scale datasets and complex tasks.

Key Techniques:

1. **Convolutional Neural Networks (CNNs)**: Effective for image and video recognition tasks.

2. **Recurrent Neural Networks (RNNs)**: Suitable for sequential data like time series and natural language.

3. **Autoencoders**: Used for unsupervised learning and dimensionality reduction.

4. **Generative Adversarial Networks (GANs)**: Consists of a generator and discriminator, used for generating realistic data.

Applications:

1. **Image and Video Analysis**: Object detection, image segmentation, facial recognition.

2. **Natural Language Processing**: Machine translation, text generation, sentiment analysis.

3. **Healthcare**: Analyzing medical images, predicting patient outcomes.

4. **Autonomous Systems**: Self-driving cars, drones.

Challenges:

1. **Data Requirements:** Deep learning models require large amounts of labeled data for training.

2. **Computational Resources:** Training deep neural networks is resource-intensive and time-consuming.

3. **Interpretability:** Deep learning models are complex and difficult to interpret, making it hard to understand their decision-making process.

Natural Language Processing (NLP)

Definition: Natural Language Processing (NLP) is a field of AI focused on the interaction between computers and human language. It involves enabling computers to understand, interpret, and generate human language in a way that is meaningful .

Components:

1. **Text Processing:** Techniques for tokenizing, parsing, and normalizing text.

2. **Language Models:** Statistical models that predict the probability of sequences of words.

3. **Machine Translation:** Automatically translating text from one language to another.

4. **Sentiment Analysis:** Determining the sentiment or emotion expressed in text.

Key Techniques:

1. **Tokenization:** Splitting text into individual words or tokens.

2. **Part-of-Speech Tagging:** Identifying the grammatical parts of speech in text.

3. **Named Entity Recognition (NER):** Identifying entities

such as names, dates, and locations in text.

4. **Word Embeddings**: Representing words as vectors in a continuous vector space (e.g., Word2Vec, GloVe).

5. **Transformers**: Advanced deep learning models for NLP tasks (e.g., BERT, GPT-3).

Applications:

1. **Chatbots**: Conversational agents that interact with users in natural language.

2. **Machine Translation**: Translating text between languages (e.g., Google Translate).

3. **Information Retrieval**: Search engines that retrieve relevant documents based on queries.

4. **Text Summarization**: Automatically generating concise summaries of longer texts.

Challenges:

1. **Ambiguity**: Human language is inherently ambiguous and context-dependent.

2. **Data Quality**: NLP models require high-quality, annotated text data for training.

3. **Multilinguality**: Handling multiple languages and dialects effectively.

Computer Vision

Definition: Computer Vision is a field of AI that enables machines to interpret and understand visual information from the world. It involves the development of algorithms and models that can process images and videos to extract meaningful information.

Key Tasks:

1. **Image Classification**: Identifying the category or class of objects in an image.
2. **Object Detection**: Locating and identifying objects within an image.
3. **Image Segmentation**: Partitioning an image into segments or regions based on features.
4. **Facial Recognition**: Identifying or verifying individuals based on facial features.
5. **Optical Character Recognition (OCR)**: Converting printed or handwritten text into machine-encoded text.

Key Techniques:

1. **Convolutional Neural Networks (CNNs)**: The backbone of most computer vision tasks, CNNs are designed to process grid-like data such as images.
2. **Feature Extraction**: Identifying and extracting important features from images.
3. **Image Preprocessing**: Techniques such as normalization, resizing, and augmentation to prepare images for analysis.
4. **Transfer Learning**: Using pre-trained models on large datasets and fine-tuning them for specific tasks.

Applications:

1. **Autonomous Vehicles**: Enabling cars to perceive and navigate their environment.
2. **Medical Imaging**: Assisting in the diagnosis of diseases by analyzing medical images.
3. **Security and Surveillance**: Monitoring and detecting suspicious activities through video feeds.
4. **Retail**: Enhancing customer experiences through visual search and product recommendations.

Challenges:

1. **Data Annotation**: Requires extensive labeled data for training models.
2. **Variability**: Handling variations in lighting, angle, and occlusion in images.
3. **Real-Time Processing**: Ensuring fast and accurate processing of visual information for applications like autonomous driving.

CHAPTER 4

AI TECHNOLOGIES AND TOOLS

Programming Languages

Python: Python is the most popular programming language for AI and machine learning due to its simplicity, readability, and extensive ecosystem of libraries and frameworks. It offers numerous libraries specifically designed for AI tasks, such as TensorFlow, PyTorch, scikit-learn, and Keras. Python's ease of use allows developers and researchers to quickly prototype and iterate on models.

Key Features:

1. **Ease of Learning and Use**: Python's syntax is clear and concise, making it accessible to both beginners and experienced programmers.

2. **Extensive Libraries**: A wide range of libraries are available for various AI tasks, from data manipulation (NumPy, Pandas) to deep learning (TensorFlow, PyTorch).

3. **Community Support**: A large, active community provides support, tutorials, and code examples.

Applications:

1. **Machine Learning**: Implementing algorithms for classification, regression, clustering, etc.

2. **Deep Learning**: Building and training neural networks for tasks like image recognition and natural language processing.

3. **Data Analysis**: Performing exploratory data analysis, visualization, and preprocessing.

R: R is another prominent programming language widely used for statistical computing and graphics. It is particularly favored in the academic and research communities for its robust statistical analysis capabilities.

Key Features:

1. **Statistical Analysis**: R excels in data analysis and statistical modeling.
2. **Visualization**: Strong capabilities for data visualization through libraries like ggplot2 and Shiny.
3. **Integration with AI**: Can integrate with TensorFlow and Keras for deep learning tasks.

Applications:

1. **Data Analysis**: Statistical analysis, hypothesis testing, and data visualization.
2. **Machine Learning**: Implementing machine learning algorithms using packages like caret and randomForest.
3. **Bioinformatics**: Analyzing biological data and conducting research in genetics and genomics.

Other Languages:

- **Java**: Used for large-scale, high-performance applications. Libraries like Weka provide machine learning capabilities.
- **C++**: Offers high performance and is used in environments where efficiency is critical. Libraries like dlib provide machine learning functions.
- **Julia**: Known for its high performance in numerical computing and its growing ecosystem for machine learning.

Frameworks and Libraries

TensorFlow: Developed by Google Brain, TensorFlow is one of the most widely used frameworks for deep learning. It provides a flexible ecosystem of tools, libraries, and community resources that enable researchers and developers to build and deploy machine learning models.

Key Features:

1. **Flexibility**: Supports both high-level APIs (like Keras) and low-level operations for fine-tuning models.
2. **Scalability**: Efficiently scales from single devices to large clusters of servers.
3. **Visualization**: TensorBoard provides robust tools for visualizing model metrics, graphs, and performance.

Applications:

1. **Image and Speech Recognition**: Building models for tasks like object detection and speech-to-text.
2. **Natural Language Processing**: Implementing models for translation, summarization, and sentiment analysis.
3. **Reinforcement Learning**: Developing agents that learn through interaction with environments.

PyTorch: Developed by Facebook's AI Research lab (FAIR), PyTorch is a popular deep learning framework known for its dynamic computation graph, which makes it easier to debug and modify models on the fly.

Key Features:

1. **Dynamic Computation Graph**: Facilitates flexibility in building and modifying neural networks.
2. **Intuitive Interface**: Provides a more Pythonic and user-friendly approach to building models.

3. **Community and Ecosystem**: A growing community with extensive tutorials, examples, and third-party libraries.

Applications:

1. **Research and Development**: Preferred in academic settings for experimenting with new models and ideas.
2. **Computer Vision**: Implementing convolutional neural networks (CNNs) for image classification and segmentation.
3. **Natural Language Processing**: Building models for language modeling, machine translation, and text generation.

scikit-learn: scikit-learn is a robust machine learning library for Python, offering simple and efficient tools for data mining and data analysis. It is built on NumPy, SciPy, and matplotlib.

Key Features:

1. **Comprehensive**: Provides a wide range of supervised and unsupervised learning algorithms.
2. **Easy to Use**: Simple and consistent API for implementing and testing models.
3. **Integration**: Easily integrates with other Python libraries for data analysis and visualization.

Applications:

1. **Data Preprocessing**: Techniques for scaling, normalization, and encoding categorical variables.
2. **Model Selection and Evaluation**: Tools for cross-validation, hyperparameter tuning, and performance metrics.
3. **Machine Learning**: Implementing algorithms for regression, classification, clustering, and dimensionality

reduction.

Keras: Keras is a high-level neural networks API, written in Python and capable of running on top of TensorFlow, Microsoft Cognitive Toolkit (CNTK), or Theano. It is designed to enable fast experimentation.

Key Features:

1. **User-Friendly**: Simplifies the process of building neural networks with an intuitive API.
2. **Modularity**: Provides modular building blocks for developing and training models.
3. **Flexibility**: Allows easy switching between different backends (TensorFlow, CNTK, Theano).

Applications:

1. **Prototyping**: Quickly building and testing neural network models.
2. **Deep Learning**: Implementing deep learning models for tasks like image recognition and natural language processing.
3. **Transfer Learning**: Fine-tuning pre-trained models on new datasets.

AI Platforms

Google AI Platform: Google AI Platform offers a comprehensive suite of machine learning services and tools on Google Cloud, designed to streamline the development, training, and deployment of machine learning models.

Key Features:

1. **AutoML**: Tools for automating the building and deployment of ML models, making it accessible to users

with limited ML expertise.

2. **TensorFlow Extended (TFX)**: End-to-end platform for deploying production machine learning pipelines.
3. **BigQuery ML**: Enables the use of SQL to build and train machine learning models directly in BigQuery.

Applications:

1. **Data Analysis and Preparation**: Leveraging Google Cloud Storage and BigQuery for data handling.
2. **Model Training and Deployment**: Using AI Platform Notebooks and AI Platform Training for scalable training and AI Platform Prediction for serving models.
3. **Automated Machine Learning**: Building models with AutoML for tasks like image classification and natural language processing.

IBM Watson: IBM Watson provides a set of AI tools and services on IBM Cloud, designed to enable businesses to integrate AI into their workflows and applications.

Key Features:

1. **Natural Language Understanding**: Tools for extracting metadata from content such as keywords, categories, and sentiment.
2. **Watson Assistant**: A platform for building and deploying conversational AI solutions.
3. **Visual Recognition**: APIs for analyzing visual content and extracting insights from images and videos.

Applications:

1. **Customer Service**: Developing chatbots and virtual assistants to enhance customer interactions.
2. **Data Analysis**: Utilizing Watson's natural language

processing capabilities for extracting insights from unstructured data.

3. **Healthcare**: Analyzing medical data to support diagnostics and treatment recommendations.

Microsoft Azure AI: Microsoft Azure AI provides a comprehensive set of AI services on the Azure cloud platform, designed to empower developers and data scientists to build intelligent applications.

Key Features:

1. **Azure Machine Learning**: A cloud-based environment for training, deploying, and managing machine learning models.

2. **Cognitive Services**: Pre-built APIs for vision, speech, language, and decision-making tasks.

3. **Bot Service**: Tools for building, testing, and deploying conversational bots.

Applications:

1. **Model Training and Deployment**: Using Azure Machine Learning for end-to-end machine learning workflows.

2. **Conversational AI**: Building intelligent bots with Azure Bot Service and integrating them with various channels.

3. **Cognitive Services**: Implementing AI capabilities like image recognition, speech-to-text, and language understanding using pre-trained models.

CHAPTER 5

APPLICATIONS OF AI

Artificial Intelligence (AI) has revolutionized numerous industries by enhancing efficiency, accuracy, and the ability to handle complex tasks. This chapter explores various applications of AI across different sectors, demonstrating its transformative impact.

Healthcare

Diagnosis: AI systems assist in diagnosing diseases by analyzing medical data, such as images, lab results, and patient records. Machine learning algorithms can identify patterns and anomalies that may indicate conditions such as cancer, heart disease, and neurological disorders.

Key Applications:

1. **Medical Imaging**: AI-powered tools analyze X-rays, MRIs, and CT scans to detect abnormalities and diseases. For example, AI algorithms can identify tumors in radiological images with high accuracy.

2. **Pathology**: AI systems assist pathologists by analyzing tissue samples to detect cancerous cells and other abnormalities.

3. **Genomics**: AI analyzes genetic data to identify mutations and predict the risk of hereditary diseases.

Personalized Medicine: AI enables personalized treatment plans tailored to individual patients based on their genetic makeup, lifestyle, and other factors. By analyzing vast amounts of data, AI systems can recommend treatments that are more likely to be effective for specific patients.

Key Applications:

1. **Predictive Analytics**: AI models predict disease progression and treatment outcomes, allowing for early intervention and tailored therapies.

2. **Drug Discovery**: AI accelerates the discovery of new drugs by analyzing biological data and predicting the efficacy of potential compounds.

3. **Patient Monitoring**: Wearable devices and AI algorithms monitor patients' vital signs in real-time, alerting healthcare providers to potential issues before they become critical.

Challenges:

1. **Data Privacy**: Ensuring the privacy and security of sensitive medical data is paramount.

2. **Bias and Fairness**: AI models must be trained on diverse datasets to avoid biases that could impact diagnosis and treatment.

3. **Regulatory Approval**: AI applications in healthcare must undergo rigorous testing and approval by regulatory bodies to ensure safety and efficacy.

Finance

Fraud Detection: AI systems detect fraudulent activities by analyzing transaction data and identifying patterns that deviate from normal behavior. Machine learning algorithms can adapt to new fraud tactics, improving detection rates and reducing false positives.

Key Applications:

1. **Credit Card Fraud**: AI models analyze transaction patterns

to detect anomalies and flag potentially fraudulent activities in real-time.

2. **Insurance Fraud**: AI systems identify fraudulent claims by analyzing historical data and detecting inconsistencies in new claims.

3. **Money Laundering**: AI algorithms monitor financial transactions to identify suspicious activities that may indicate money laundering.

Algorithmic Trading: AI-driven trading systems analyze market data and execute trades based on predefined strategies. These systems can process vast amounts of data much faster than human traders, identifying profitable opportunities and minimizing risks.

Key Applications:

1. **High-Frequency Trading**: AI algorithms execute a large number of trades at high speeds, capitalizing on small price movements.

2. **Quantitative Trading**: AI models analyze historical data and market trends to develop trading strategies that optimize returns.

3. **Risk Management**: AI systems assess and manage financial risks by analyzing market conditions and predicting potential downturns.

Challenges:

1. **Market Volatility**: AI models must be robust enough to handle sudden market changes and volatility.

2. **Regulatory Compliance**: Ensuring that AI-driven trading systems comply with financial regulations is crucial.

3. **Transparency**: The decision-making processes of AI algorithms must be transparent to gain the trust of regulators and investors.

Transportation

Autonomous Vehicles: AI is at the core of self-driving technology, enabling vehicles to navigate roads, interpret traffic signals, and make real-time decisions. Autonomous vehicles use sensors, cameras, and AI algorithms to understand their environment and operate safely.

Key Applications:

1. **Self-Driving Cars**: Companies like Tesla, Waymo, and Uber are developing autonomous vehicles that can drive with little to no human intervention.

2. **Fleet Management**: AI systems optimize the management of vehicle fleets, improving route planning, fuel efficiency, and maintenance schedules.

3. **Public Transportation**: AI enhances the efficiency and safety of public transportation systems, including buses, trains, and subways.

Traffic Management: AI optimizes traffic flow in urban areas by analyzing data from traffic sensors, cameras, and GPS devices. AI systems can predict traffic congestion and suggest alternative routes to drivers, reducing travel times and emissions.

Key Applications:

1. **Smart Traffic Lights**: AI algorithms adjust traffic light timings based on real-time traffic conditions, improving traffic flow and reducing waiting times.

2. **Incident Detection**: AI systems monitor traffic cameras and sensors to detect accidents or breakdowns, alerting

authorities and directing traffic accordingly.

3. **Predictive Maintenance**: AI predicts when traffic infrastructure, such as roads and bridges, will need maintenance, preventing costly repairs and improving safety.

Challenges:

1. **Safety and Reliability**: Ensuring the safety and reliability of autonomous vehicles and AI-driven traffic systems is critical.

2. **Regulatory and Legal Issues**: Developing regulations and legal frameworks to govern the use of AI in transportation is necessary.

3. **Public Acceptance**: Gaining public trust and acceptance of autonomous vehicles and AI-driven traffic management systems is essential for widespread adoption.

Entertainment

Recommendation Systems: AI-powered recommendation systems personalize content for users based on their preferences and behavior. These systems analyze user data to suggest movies, music, books, and other content that users are likely to enjoy.

Key Applications:

1. **Streaming Services**: Platforms like Netflix, Spotify, and YouTube use AI algorithms to recommend movies, music, and videos to users.

2. **E-commerce**: Online retailers like Amazon use AI to recommend products based on user browsing and purchase history.

3. **Social Media**: AI curates content on social media platforms,

suggesting posts, friends, and advertisements that match user interests.

Game AI: AI enhances the gaming experience by creating intelligent and responsive non-player characters (NPCs) and by adapting game difficulty based on player performance. Game AI can also be used to generate new game content procedurally.

Key Applications:

1. **NPC Behavior**: AI algorithms control the actions of NPCs, making them more lifelike and challenging for players.

2. **Procedural Content Generation**: AI generates game levels, characters, and storylines, adding variety and replayability to games.

3. **Player Experience**: AI adjusts game difficulty and content based on player behavior and skill level, providing a personalized gaming experience.

Challenges:

1. **Data Privacy**: Protecting user data and ensuring privacy in AI-driven recommendation systems is crucial.

2. **Bias and Fairness**: AI algorithms must be designed to avoid biases that could impact recommendations or game behavior.

3. **Ethical Considerations**: Ensuring ethical use of AI in entertainment, such as avoiding addictive designs and respecting user autonomy.

Customer Service

Chatbots: AI-powered chatbots provide 24/7 customer support by handling routine inquiries and tasks. These chatbots use natural language processing (NLP) to understand and respond to customer queries, improving response times and customer satisfaction.

Key Applications:

1. **Customer Support**: Chatbots handle common customer inquiries, such as account information, order status, and troubleshooting.

2. **Sales and Marketing**: AI chatbots engage with potential customers, providing product information and assisting with purchases.

3. **Appointment Scheduling**: Chatbots help schedule appointments and reminders, streamlining the process for businesses and customers.

Virtual Assistants: Virtual assistants like Siri, Alexa, and Google Assistant use AI to perform tasks such as setting reminders, sending messages, and controlling smart home devices. These assistants understand natural language commands and interact with users in a conversational manner.

Key Applications:

1. **Home Automation**: Controlling smart home devices, such as lights, thermostats, and security systems.

2. **Personal Productivity**: Managing calendars, setting reminders, and providing weather and traffic updates.

3. **Information Retrieval**: Answering questions, providing news updates, and retrieving information from the internet.

Challenges:

1. **Natural Language Understanding**: Improving the accuracy and understanding of AI systems in interpreting natural language queries.

2. **Data Security**: Ensuring the security and privacy of user data handled by chatbots and virtual assistants.

3. **User Trust**: Building and maintaining trust with users by providing reliable and accurate responses.

CHAPTER 6

ETHICAL CONSIDERATIONS OF AI

As Artificial Intelligence (AI) technologies continue to evolve and integrate into various aspects of society, it becomes increasingly important to address the ethical implications associated with their development and use. Ethical considerations in AI encompass a range of issues, including bias and fairness, privacy, job displacement, and accountability. This section delves into each of these critical areas to highlight the challenges and necessary measures to ensure the responsible use of AI.

Bias and Fairness

Definition: Bias in AI refers to the presence of systematic and unfair discrimination in the outcomes of AI systems. Fairness involves ensuring that these systems treat all individuals and groups equitably.

Challenges:

1. **Data Bias**: AI systems learn from data, and if the training data contains biases, these biases can be perpetuated and even amplified in the AI's decisions and predictions. For example, historical data reflecting gender or racial biases

can lead to discriminatory outcomes.

2. **Algorithmic Bias**: The design and implementation of algorithms can introduce bias. This can occur through the choice of features, the structure of the model, or even through inadvertent programming errors.

Strategies to Mitigate Bias:

1. **Diverse Datasets**: Ensuring that training data is representative of all demographic groups to prevent skewed outcomes.

2. **Bias Audits**: Regularly auditing AI systems for bias using statistical methods and fairness metrics.

3. **Transparent Algorithms**: Developing transparent and interpretable models to understand and address sources of bias.

4. **Ethical Guidelines**: Establishing ethical guidelines and frameworks for AI development that prioritize fairness and equity.

Examples:

1. **Hiring Systems**: AI used in recruitment can inadvertently favor certain groups over others if trained on biased historical hiring data.

2. **Credit Scoring**: AI models used for credit scoring can discriminate against certain socioeconomic groups if not properly designed and monitored.

Privacy

Definition: Privacy in AI involves protecting individuals' personal data and ensuring that it is handled responsibly throughout the AI system's lifecycle.

Challenges:

1. **Data Collection**: AI systems often require vast amounts of data, which can include sensitive personal information. Collecting and storing this data poses significant privacy risks.

2. **Data Sharing**: Sharing data across organizations or with third parties can increase the risk of privacy breaches.

3. **Data Usage**: Ensuring that data is used only for the intended purposes and not exploited for unauthorized activities.

Strategies to Protect Privacy:

1. **Data Anonymization**: Removing personally identifiable information from datasets to protect individual privacy.

2. **Consent Mechanisms**: Implementing clear and transparent consent mechanisms to inform users about how their data will be used and obtaining their explicit consent.

3. **Data Minimization**: Collecting only the data that is necessary for the AI system to function, reducing the risk of privacy violations.

4. **Secure Data Storage**: Using encryption and other security measures to protect data from unauthorized access and breaches.

Examples:

1. **Healthcare**: AI systems used in healthcare must protect patient data and comply with regulations like HIPAA (Health Insurance Portability and Accountability Act).

2. **Social Media**: AI algorithms on social media platforms must handle user data responsibly to prevent misuse and ensure user privacy.

Job Displacement

Definition: Job displacement refers to the impact of AI on employment, where AI systems and automation replace human workers in certain tasks and roles.

Challenges:

1. **Economic Disruption**: The widespread adoption of AI and automation can lead to significant economic disruption, with certain jobs becoming obsolete.

2. **Skill Mismatch**: The skills required for AI-related jobs may not match the current workforce's skill set, leading to a gap in employment opportunities.

Strategies to Address Job Displacement:

1. **Reskilling and Upskilling**: Providing training programs to help workers acquire new skills that are in demand in an AI-driven economy.

2. **Job Transition Support**: Offering support services such as career counseling, job placement assistance, and financial aid to workers affected by AI-driven changes.

3. **Policy Measures**: Implementing policies that promote job creation in sectors that are less likely to be automated and encouraging the growth of industries that can absorb displaced workers.

Examples:

1. **Manufacturing**: Automation in manufacturing can lead to job losses for assembly line workers but create new opportunities in robotics maintenance and programming.

2. **Customer Service**: Chatbots and virtual assistants may reduce the need for human customer service representatives,

but new jobs can emerge in AI training and management.

Accountability

Definition: Accountability in AI involves determining who is responsible for the decisions made by AI systems and ensuring that these systems operate transparently and ethically.

Challenges:

1. **Complex Decision-Making**: AI systems often make decisions based on complex algorithms and large datasets, making it difficult to trace the decision-making process.

2. **Lack of Transparency**: Many AI models, particularly deep learning models, operate as "black boxes," where the reasoning behind decisions is not easily understood.

3. **Shared Responsibility**: The development and deployment of AI systems typically involve multiple stakeholders, including developers, data providers, and users, complicating the assignment of responsibility.

Strategies to Ensure Accountability:

1. **Explainable AI**: Developing AI models that provide clear and understandable explanations for their decisions, enabling users to understand and trust the system.

2. **Regulatory Frameworks**: Establishing regulations that define the responsibilities and liabilities of different stakeholders involved in AI development and deployment.

3. **Ethical Audits**: Conducting regular audits of AI systems to ensure they comply with ethical standards and regulations.

4. **Clear Governance Structures**: Implementing governance structures within organizations to oversee AI projects and ensure accountability.

Examples:

1. **Autonomous Vehicles**: Determining responsibility in case of an accident involving an autonomous vehicle, whether it lies with the manufacturer, the software developer, or the owner.

2. **Financial Algorithms**: Holding financial institutions accountable for the decisions made by AI-driven trading algorithms that can impact markets and investors.

CHAPTER 7

FUTURE OF AI

The future of Artificial Intelligence (AI) is a topic of great interest and importance as it holds the potential to transform nearly every aspect of our lives. This section explores current trends in AI research and applications, the challenges that need to be addressed, and the opportunities that AI presents for the future.

Current Trends

Advances in AI Research and Applications: The field of AI is rapidly evolving, with continuous advancements in research and applications. Some of the most notable trends include:

1. **Deep Learning and Neural Networks**:
   - **Advancements**: Deep learning, a subset of machine learning, continues to make significant strides. Researchers are developing more complex neural network architectures, such as transformer models, which have achieved state-of-the-art performance in natural language processing tasks.
   - **Applications**: These advancements are being applied in various fields, including image recognition, language translation, and autonomous systems.

2. **Natural Language Processing (NLP)**:
   - **Advancements**: NLP technologies have improved dramatically with the development of models like

BERT, GPT-3, and their successors. These models can understand and generate human language with high accuracy and fluency.

- o **Applications**: NLP is used in chatbots, virtual assistants, sentiment analysis, and automated content generation.

3. **Reinforcement Learning**:
- o **Advancements**: Reinforcement learning algorithms, which learn through trial and error, have achieved remarkable success in complex tasks such as playing games and robotic control.
- o **Applications**: This technology is being used in autonomous vehicles, robotics, and optimization problems.

4. **AI in Healthcare**:
- o **Advancements**: AI is making significant contributions to healthcare through predictive analytics, personalized medicine, and advanced diagnostics.
- o **Applications**: AI-powered tools assist in diagnosing diseases, recommending treatments, and predicting patient outcomes.

5. **Edge AI**:
- o **Advancements**: Edge AI refers to the deployment of AI models on edge devices, such as smartphones and IoT devices, rather than in centralized data centers.
- o **Applications**: This trend enables real-time processing and decision-making in applications like

autonomous drones, smart home devices, and wearable health monitors.

6. **Ethical AI**:

   o **Advancements**: There is a growing focus on developing AI systems that are ethical, transparent, and fair. Researchers are working on algorithms that mitigate bias and improve interpretability.

   o **Applications**: Ethical AI principles are being integrated into various applications to ensure responsible use.

Challenges

Technical, Ethical, and Societal Challenges:

1. **Technical Challenges**:

   o **Data Quality and Availability**: High-quality, labeled data is essential for training AI models. Obtaining and maintaining such datasets can be difficult and expensive.

   o **Scalability**: As AI models become more complex, they require significant computational resources, which can be a barrier for smaller organizations.

   o **Interpretability**: Many AI models, especially deep learning models, operate as "black boxes," making it challenging to understand and trust their decisions.

2. **Ethical Challenges**:

   o **Bias and Fairness**: AI systems can perpetuate and amplify existing biases present in training data. Ensuring fairness and avoiding discrimination is a significant challenge.

o **Privacy**: AI systems often require large amounts of personal data, raising concerns about data privacy and security.

o **Transparency**: There is a need for transparency in AI decision-making processes to build trust and accountability.

3. **Societal Challenges**:

o **Job Displacement**: The automation of tasks by AI systems can lead to job losses and economic disruption. Preparing the workforce for this transition is crucial.

o **Social Inequality**: AI technology could exacerbate social inequalities if its benefits are not distributed equitably.

o **Regulation and Governance**: Establishing effective regulations and governance structures to oversee AI development and deployment is essential to address ethical and societal concerns.

Opportunities
Potential Benefits and Breakthroughs:

1. **Enhanced Productivity and Efficiency**:

o **Automation**: AI can automate repetitive and mundane tasks, allowing humans to focus on more complex and creative work. This can lead to significant productivity gains across various industries.

o **Optimization**: AI algorithms can optimize

processes in manufacturing, logistics, and supply chain management, reducing costs and improving efficiency.

2. **Improved Healthcare**:
   o **Personalized Medicine**: AI can analyze genetic and clinical data to provide personalized treatment plans, improving patient outcomes.
   o **Predictive Analytics**: AI-powered predictive analytics can help in early detection of diseases, preventing complications and reducing healthcare costs.

3. **Advanced Scientific Research**:
   o **Drug Discovery**: AI accelerates drug discovery by predicting the effectiveness of compounds and identifying potential new drugs.
   o **Climate Modeling**: AI helps in modeling and predicting climate change impacts, aiding in the development of mitigation and adaptation strategies.

4. **Enhanced Customer Experience**:
   o **Personalization**: AI enables highly personalized experiences in e-commerce, entertainment, and social media, increasing customer satisfaction and engagement.
   o **Customer Support**: AI-powered chatbots and virtual assistants provide 24/7 support, improving response times and customer service quality.

5. **Sustainable Development**:
   o **Energy Management**: AI optimizes energy

consumption in smart grids, reducing waste and promoting sustainable energy use.

o **Agriculture**: AI-driven precision agriculture techniques improve crop yields and resource management, contributing to food security.

6. **Education and Learning**:

o **Personalized Learning**: AI can tailor educational content to individual students' needs, enhancing learning outcomes.

o **Tutoring Systems**: AI-powered tutoring systems provide personalized assistance and feedback, supporting students in their learning journey.

7. **Safety and Security**:

o **Cybersecurity**: AI enhances cybersecurity by detecting and responding to threats in real-time, protecting data and systems from attacks.

o **Public Safety**: AI systems assist in monitoring and responding to public safety threats, such as natural disasters and crime.

The future of AI holds immense promise, with ongoing advancements poised to transform various sectors and improve our daily lives. However, realizing the full potential of AI requires addressing significant technical, ethical, and societal challenges. By promoting responsible development and equitable distribution of AI technologies, we can harness their benefits while mitigating risks. The future of AI is not just about technological progress but also about creating a more inclusive, fair, and sustainable world.

CHAPTER 8

GLOSSARY OF AI TERMS

Glossary of AI Terms

This glossary provides brief definitions of common terms and concepts in Artificial Intelligence (AI). Understanding these terms is essential for anyone studying or working in the field of AI.

1. Artificial Intelligence (AI): The branch of computer science focused on creating systems capable of performing tasks that typically require human intelligence, such as reasoning, learning, problem-solving, perception, and language understanding.

2. Machine Learning (ML): A subset of AI that involves training algorithms to learn from and make predictions or decisions based on data. It emphasizes the development of models that improve their performance over time without being explicitly programmed.

3. Supervised Learning: A type of machine learning where the algorithm is trained on labeled data. Each training example includes input-output pairs, and the algorithm learns to map inputs to the correct outputs.

4. Unsupervised Learning: A type of machine learning where the algorithm is trained on unlabeled data. The goal is to identify patterns, structures, or relationships within the data without explicit guidance on what the output should be.

5. Reinforcement Learning (RL): A type of machine learning where an agent learns to make decisions by performing actions in an environment to maximize cumulative rewards. The agent receives feedback in the form of rewards or punishments and adjusts its actions accordingly.

6. Neural Networks: A class of machine learning models inspired by the structure and function of the human brain. They consist of interconnected layers of artificial neurons that process data and learn to perform tasks through training.

7. Deep Learning: A subset of machine learning that involves neural networks with many layers (deep neural networks). It is particularly effective for tasks involving large amounts of data and complex patterns, such as image and speech recognition.

8. Natural Language Processing (NLP): A field of AI focused on the interaction between computers and human language. It involves enabling computers to understand, interpret, and generate human language in a meaningful way.

9. Computer Vision: A field of AI that enables machines to interpret and understand visual information from the world. It involves developing algorithms and models that can process images and videos to extract meaningful information.

10. Algorithm: A step-by-step procedure or formula for solving a problem. In AI, algorithms are used to perform tasks such as classification, regression, clustering, and optimization.

11. Artificial General Intelligence (AGI): A theoretical level of AI where machines possess the ability to understand, learn, and apply knowledge across a wide range of tasks at a level comparable to human intelligence.

12. Superintelligent AI: A level of AI that surpasses the smartest and most gifted human minds. It involves AI systems that significantly exceed human cognitive capabilities across all areas.

13. Bias: The presence of systematic and unfair discrimination in the outcomes of AI systems. Bias can arise from training data, algorithms, or human input, and it can lead to discriminatory practices.

14. Fairness: Ensuring that AI systems treat all individuals and groups equitably, without discrimination. Fairness involves addressing and mitigating biases to promote ethical and just outcomes.

15. Privacy: The protection of individuals' personal data and ensuring that it is handled responsibly. Privacy concerns in AI involve the collection, storage, and usage of sensitive data.

16. Job Displacement: The impact of AI on employment, where AI systems and automation replace human workers in certain tasks and roles. It raises concerns about economic disruption and the need for reskilling and upskilling the workforce.

17. Accountability: Determining who is responsible for the decisions made by AI systems. Accountability involves ensuring that AI operates transparently and ethically, with clear governance structures.

18. Data Quality: The accuracy, completeness, and reliability of data used to train AI models. High-quality data is essential for the performance and fairness of AI systems.

19. Scalability: The ability of an AI system to handle increasing amounts of data or complexity without compromising performance. Scalability is crucial for deploying AI solutions in real-world scenarios.

20. Interpretability: The extent to which the internal workings of an AI model can be understood by humans. Interpretability is important for building trust and ensuring that AI decisions are transparent.

21. Transparency: The openness and clarity with which AI systems operate. Transparency involves providing insights into how AI models make decisions and the data they use.

22. Explainable AI (XAI): AI systems designed to provide clear and understandable explanations for their decisions. XAI aims to make AI models more transparent and interpretable.

23. Data Anonymization: The process of removing personally identifiable information from datasets to protect individual privacy. Anonymization helps ensure that data can be used for analysis without compromising privacy.

24. Data Minimization: The principle of collecting only the data that is necessary for a specific purpose, reducing the risk of privacy violations and data misuse.

25. Encryption: A method of securing data by converting it into a coded format that can only be read by authorized parties. Encryption is crucial for protecting sensitive data from unauthorized access.

26. Transfer Learning: A machine learning technique where a pre-trained model on one task is adapted for use on a different but related task. Transfer learning leverages existing knowledge to improve performance on new tasks.

27. Feature Extraction: The process of identifying and extracting relevant features from raw data to use as input for machine learning models. Feature extraction is crucial for improving model accuracy and efficiency.

28. Hyperparameter Tuning: The process of optimizing the hyperparameters of a machine learning model to improve its performance. Hyperparameters are settings that control the training process and model complexity.

29. Overfitting: A situation where a machine learning model performs well on training data but poorly on new, unseen data. Overfitting occurs when the model learns noise and details specific to the training data rather than general patterns.

30. Underfitting: A situation where a machine learning model is too simple to capture the underlying patterns in the data. Underfitting leads to poor performance on both training and new data.

31. Cross-Validation: A technique for assessing the performance of a machine learning model by dividing the data into multiple subsets and training/testing the model on different combinations. Cross-validation helps prevent overfitting and provides a more accurate evaluation.

32. Gradient Descent: An optimization algorithm used to minimize the loss function in machine learning models. Gradient descent iteratively adjusts the model parameters to find the optimal solution.

33. Loss Function: A mathematical function that measures the difference between the predicted output of a model and the actual target value. The loss function guides the optimization process during training.

34. Activation Function: A function applied to the output of a neuron in a neural network to introduce non-linearity. Common activation functions include ReLU (Rectified Linear Unit), Sigmoid, and Tanh.

35. Convolutional Neural Networks (CNNs): A type of neural network designed for processing grid-like data, such as images. CNNs use convolutional layers to automatically learn spatial hierarchies of features.

36. Recurrent Neural Networks (RNNs): A type of neural network designed for sequential data, such as time series and text. RNNs have connections that form directed cycles, allowing them to maintain memory of previous inputs.

37. Long Short-Term Memory (LSTM): A type of RNN that addresses the vanishing gradient problem, making it suitable for learning long-term dependencies in sequential data.

38. Generative Adversarial Networks (GANs): A class of machine learning models consisting of two neural networks—a generator and a discriminator—that compete against each other. GANs are used for generating realistic synthetic data.

39. Autoencoders: A type of neural network used for unsupervised learning and dimensionality reduction. Autoencoders learn to encode data into a lower-dimensional representation and then decode it back to the original form.

40. Principal Component Analysis (PCA): A statistical technique for dimensionality reduction that transforms data into a new set of orthogonal variables (principal components) that capture the most variance.

41. Clustering: An unsupervised learning technique for grouping data points into clusters based on their similarities. Common clustering algorithms include K-Means, Hierarchical Clustering, and DBSCAN.

42. Association Rule Learning: A machine learning technique for discovering interesting relationships between variables in large datasets. It is commonly used in market basket analysis.

43. Markov Decision Process (MDP): A mathematical framework for modeling decision-making problems, where outcomes are partly random and partly under the control of a decision-maker. MDPs are used in reinforcement learning.

44. Policy Gradient Methods: A family of reinforcement learning algorithms that optimize the policy directly by using gradient ascent on expected rewards.

45. Named Entity Recognition (NER): A natural language processing task that involves identifying and classifying named entities (e.g., names, dates, locations) in text.

46. Tokenization: The process of splitting text into individual words or tokens. Tokenization is a fundamental step in natural language processing.

47. Part-of-Speech Tagging (POS Tagging): The process of labeling words in text with their corresponding parts of speech (e.g., nouns, verbs, adjectives).

48. Word Embeddings: A representation of words in a continuous vector space where words with similar meanings are positioned close to each other. Common techniques for generating word embeddings include Word2Vec and GloVe.

49. Transformers: A type of deep learning model designed for handling sequential data, particularly in natural language processing. Transformers use self-attention mechanisms to capture relationships between words in a sentence. Notable transformer models include BERT and GPT-3.

50. Optical Character Recognition (OCR): The technology for converting different types of documents, such as scanned paper documents, PDFs, or images, into editable and searchable data.

51. Predictive Maintenance: Using AI and machine learning to predict equipment failures and perform maintenance proactively. This approach helps in reducing downtime and extending the life of equipment.

52. Precision Agriculture: The use of AI and other technologies to optimize agricultural practices by monitoring crop health, soil conditions, and environmental factors. Precision agriculture aims to increase yield and reduce resource usage.

53. Smart Grids: Electrical grids that use AI and other technologies to monitor and manage the production, distribution, and consumption of electricity more efficiently.

54. Autonomous Systems: Systems that can perform tasks without human intervention by using AI to perceive their environment, make decisions, and act accordingly. Examples include autonomous vehicles and drones.

55. Explainable AI (XAI): AI systems designed to provide clear and understandable explanations for their decisions. Explainable AI aims to make AI models more transparent and interpretable.

56. Big Data: Extremely large datasets that require advanced methods and technologies to store, process, and analyze. Big Data is often associated with AI because of the need for vast amounts of data to train machine learning models.

57. Internet of Things (IoT): A network of interconnected devices that collect and exchange data. AI is often used to analyze IoT data to provide insights and enable intelligent decision-making.

58. Cybersecurity: The use of AI to enhance the security of computer systems and networks by detecting and responding to threats in real-time.

59. Smart Assistants: AI-powered assistants, such as Siri, Alexa, and Google Assistant, that perform tasks and provide information based on user commands.

60. Chatbots: AI programs designed to simulate conversation with human users, often used in customer service to handle routine inquiries and provide support.

Conclusion

As we conclude this comprehensive handbook on the basics of Artificial Intelligence, it is evident that AI is a dynamic and transformative field with the potential to revolutionize various aspects of our lives. From understanding the foundational concepts and technologies to exploring the ethical considerations and future trends, this book has provided a thorough introduction to AI. We began with the definition and significance of AI, tracing its history and differentiating between types like Narrow AI, General AI, and Superintelligent AI. We then delved into the core concepts of machine learning, including supervised and unsupervised learning, reinforcement learning, neural networks, and deep learning, alongside critical applications such as natural language processing and computer vision.

Our journey also covered essential technologies and tools, highlighting programming languages like Python and R, frameworks such as TensorFlow and PyTorch, and AI platforms including Google AI, IBM Watson, and Microsoft Azure AI. We explored how AI is being applied across industries, from healthcare and finance to transportation, entertainment, and customer service, showcasing its current impact and potential for future innovations. Additionally, we addressed vital ethical considerations, including bias and fairness, privacy, job displacement, and accountability, emphasizing the need for responsible AI development and use.

Looking ahead, we discussed the current trends, challenges, and opportunities in AI, recognizing the continuous advancements and the vast possibilities they bring. Whether you are a student, researcher, developer, or AI enthusiast, this handbook serves as a foundation for further exploration and understanding. The field of

AI is ever-evolving, offering endless opportunities for learning and innovation. As you embark on your AI journey, remain curious, stay informed, and contribute to the responsible and ethical advancement of AI technologies. Wishing you the best in your endeavors to harness the power of AI and make a positive impact on the world.

www.ingramcontent.com/pod-product-compliance
Lightning Source LLC
LaVergne TN
LVHW051612050326
832903LV00033B/4467